MW00852033

DISCARD

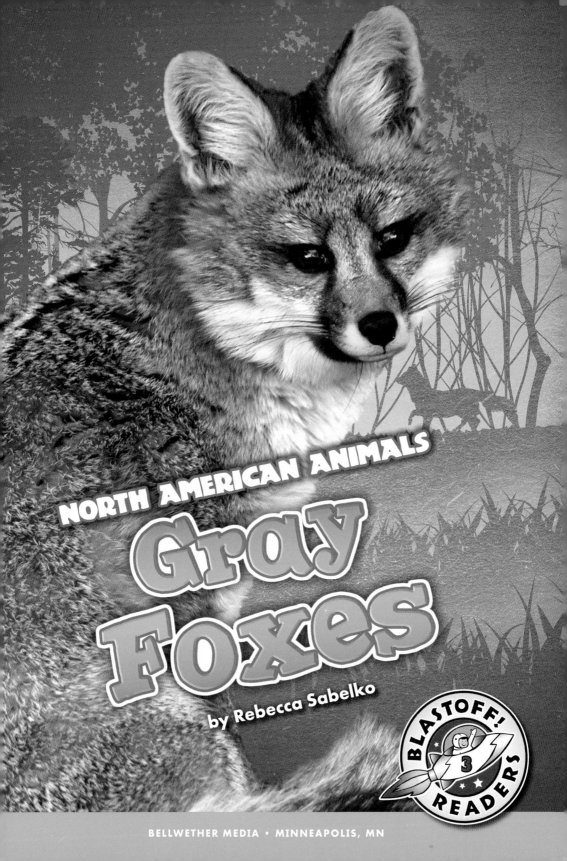

NORTH AMERICAN ANIMALS
Gray Foxes

by Rebecca Sabelko

BLASTOFF! READERS
3

BELLWETHER MEDIA • MINNEAPOLIS, MN

Note to Librarians, Teachers, and Parents:

Blastoff! Readers are carefully developed by literacy experts and combine standards-based content with developmentally appropriate text.

Level 1 provides the most support through repetition of high-frequency words, light text, predictable sentence patterns, and strong visual support.

Level 2 offers early readers a bit more challenge through varied simple sentences, increased text load, and less repetition of high-frequency words.

Level 3 advances early-fluent readers toward fluency through increased text and concept load, less reliance on visuals, longer sentences, and more literary language.

Level 4 builds reading stamina by providing more text per page, increased use of punctuation, greater variation in sentence patterns, and increasingly challenging vocabulary.

Level 5 encourages children to move from "learning to read" to "reading to learn" by providing even more text, varied writing styles, and less familiar topics.

Whichever book is right for your reader, Blastoff! Readers are the perfect books to build confidence and encourage a love of reading that will last a lifetime!

This edition first published in 2019 by Bellwether Media, Inc.

No part of this publication may be reproduced in whole or in part without written permission of the publisher. For information regarding permission, write to Bellwether Media, Inc., Attention: Permissions Department, 6012 Blue Circle Drive, Minnetonka, MN 55343.

Library of Congress Cataloging-in-Publication Data

Names: Sabelko, Rebecca, author.
Title: Gray Foxes / by Rebecca Sabelko.
Description: Minneapolis, MN : Bellwether Media, Inc., 2019. | Series: Blastoff! Readers. North American Animals | Audience: Age 5-8. | Audience: K to Grade 3. | Includes bibliographical references and index.
Identifiers: LCCN 2018030414 (print) | LCCN 2018032373 (ebook) | ISBN 9781681036434 (ebook) | ISBN 9781626179127 (hardcover : alk. paper)
Subjects: LCSH: Gray fox–Juvenile literature.
Classification: LCC QL737.C22 (ebook) | LCC QL737.C22 S23 2019 (print) | DDC 599.776–dc23
LC record available at https://lccn.loc.gov/2018030414

Editor: Kate Moening   Designer: Josh Brink

Printed in the United States of America, North Mankato, MN.

Table of Contents

What Are Gray Foxes?

Gray foxes are **mammals** that are members of the dog family. They live in many **habitats** across North America.

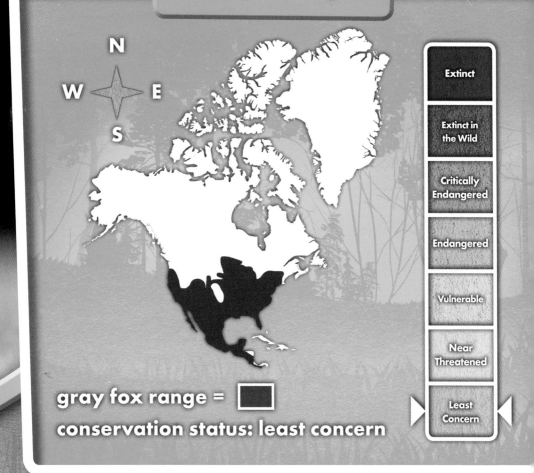

In the Wild

N
W — E
S

Extinct

Extinct in the Wild

Critically Endangered

Endangered

Vulnerable

Near Threatened

Least Concern

gray fox range = ▮
conservation status: least concern

They wander the **shrublands** and forests of the United States. They are also found throughout **Central America**.

Gray foxes prefer to live where woodlands and fields meet. They are never far from a pond or stream.

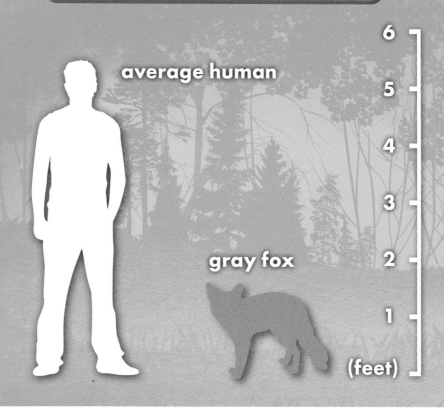

Size of a Gray Fox

average human

gray fox

6
5
4
3
2
1
(feet)

These small animals are about
30 inches (76 centimeters) long.
They live in logs or under rocks.
Some dig **dens** underground.

Gray foxes have gray fur along their backs and tails. The tips of their tails are black.

Identify a Gray Fox

black-tipped tail

short legs

retractable claws

These foxes may have a mix of white, red, and black fur on their faces and bellies.

Gray foxes have sharp, **retractable** claws. These help the foxes dig, hunt, and stay safe from **predators**.

Their special claws also help them climb. They are the only foxes that can climb trees!

retractable claws

Gray foxes are quick.
They creep up on mice and
rabbits. Then, they **pounce**!

**fruit of
California palms**

**American
grasshoppers**

cotton rats

deer mice

Eastern cottontails

ruffed grouse

These **omnivores** will also eat nuts, berries, and grains. They are not picky eaters!

Sometimes, gray foxes store extra food. They use their front paws to bury what they do not eat.

They mark the area using **scent glands** on their paws and tails. This tells other animals to stay away!

bobcats

golden eagles

great horned owls

coyotes

Gray foxes are often hunted by coyotes and **raptors**. But their fur keeps them hidden in brown leaves and bushes.

They climb trees to escape
from most land predators.

Pouncing Pups

Males and females meet in late winter. Females search for a den while males hunt. Soon, baby foxes are born! Moms **nurse** the **pups** and dads continue to find food.

Name for babies:	pups
Size of litter:	about 4 pups
Length of pregnancy:	about 2 months
Time spent with parents:	8 to 10 months

In a few weeks, the pups learn to hunt! Dad teaches them how to creep up and pounce on **prey**.

The pups grow and become skillful predators. They are ready to find a new home!

Glossary

Central America—the narrow, southern part of North America

dens—sheltered places

habitats—lands with certain types of plants, animals, and weather

mammals—warm-blooded animals that have backbones and feed their young milk

nurse—to feed babies milk

omnivores—animals that eat both plants and animals

pounce—to suddenly jump onto something to catch it

predators—animals that hunt other animals for food

prey—animals that are hunted by other animals for food

pups—baby gray foxes

raptors—large birds that hunt other animals; raptors have excellent eyesight and powerful talons.

retractable—can be pulled back in

scent glands—special organs in the body that let out smells

shrublands—dry lands that have mostly low plants and few trees

To Learn More

AT THE LIBRARY

Borgert-Spaniol, Megan. *Red Foxes*. Minneapolis, Minn.: Bellwether Media, 2015.

Bowman, Chris. *Coyotes*. Minneapolis, Minn.: Bellwether Media, 2016.

Kopp, Megan. *The Language of Dogs and Other Canines*. New York, N.Y.: Cavendish Square Publishing, 2017.

ON THE WEB

FACTSURFER

Factsurfer.com gives you a safe, fun way to find more information.

1. Go to www.factsurfer.com.

2. Enter "gray foxes" into the search box.

3. Click the "Surf" button and select your book cover to see a list of related web sites.

Index

The images in this book are reproduced through the courtesy of: milehightraveler, front cover; Exactostock-1598, pp. 4-5; Lynn_Bystrom, p. 6; sunsinger, p. 7; zhuclear, p. 8; Geoffrey Kuchera, pp. 9 (all), 10, 11, 14, 17; Warren Metcalf, p. 12; Wollertz, p. 13 (top left); Ron Hood, p. 13 (top right); Steve Byland, p. 13 (middle left); Studio DMM Photography, Designs & Art, p. 13 (middle right); CLS Digital Arts, p. 13 (bottom left); Tom Reichner, p. 13 (bottom right); Jouko van der Kruijssen/ Getty Images, p. 15; Don Mammoser, p. 16 (top left); Vladimir Kogan Michael, p. 16 (top right); Eric Isselee, p. 16 (bottom left); Cynthia Kidwell, p. 16 (bottom right); Morales, p. 18; Hemis/ Alamy, p. 19; Don Johnston/ Alamy, p. 20; mauritius images GmbH/ Alamy, p. 21.

5